Breaking Barriers:
The Journey

Jeanice B. Thomas

Life is only a journey.
Embrace it and trust God.

Always
Jean Thomas

Dedication

This book is dedicated to my children and to my loving parents, John and Marline Brown, who always encouraged me to do my best. Thanks Mom and Dad.

Acknowledgement

I thank Jesus Christ for bringing me through this journey and for allowing me to live to share this story. I thank my husband for his endless support while I wrote this book. I thank Dameron Jones for taking the time to share her editing and proofreading skills. I am forever grateful for all of the advice and formatting expertise that I received from author and instructor Meredith Bond. I also thank my wonderful friends for their encouragement and for patiently waiting for this book to be completed.

Table of Contents

Preface

WHY *was this book written?*

I never imagined that I would ever write a book—especially one about my past childhood experiences. I always thought that those experiences would be buried, at least that is what I had hoped. I never thought that my past would be shared with anyone. But something kept tugging at me to openly share those experiences with others. Being that I have always been a private type of person, I found it very difficult at first to openly share the challenges that I faced as I was growing up—since many of these challenges brought back memories of hurt and pain. I just did not want anyone to know. I have learned over the years, however, that God sometimes lets us experience things so that we can help someone else go through similar experiences. So, I decided to sit down, to listen to God, and to write this book.

At first I thought that this book would be written for the youth—to encourage them during the times in their lives when everything seems to be going wrong. You know, during those times when you may be feeling down because you have been mistreated or rejected in life. However, God led me to write this book for anyone who may be perceived as *different* —no matter if you are young or old, tall or short, shy or out-going, overweight or not, or male or female. This book is written to offer encouragement to those who feel that life is a challenge or is beating up on them because they dared to take a stand for what they felt was right.

As you read this book, please keep in mind that the experiences being shared are purposely expressed from a child's perspective to emphasize simplicity. In addition, this book is written to be an easy read.

For the readers, like myself, who like to flip to the back of the book first to see the ending, I will save you some time. The last chapter of this book is intentionally numbered as *Chapter 1* and is entitled *The Beginning of a New Journey* . This was not done to prevent you from finding out the end result, but to let you know that from the experiences shared in the previous chapters, it is indeed a new beginning—the start of new experiences that are deeply rooted from my childhood lessons. May you find encouragement from this book and may God bless you while reading it.

Introduction

I was born in Suffolk, a quiet rural town in Virginia, mostly known at that time for its peanut farms. Like most towns in the South, everyone practically knew each other, or at least thought that they did. My parents were considered as the working middle-class, which really meant that they had to work very hard to keep what they had. Their way of living, though simple, was better than their parents'. It was how life was supposed to be.

My parents always used to say to me when I was growing up, "Whatever you do in life, keep it honest and always strive to do your best." So, I tried to follow their advice, as best as I knew how, which was easier said than done. As a child, there were many things that I just did not understand, and at times I did not even know how to express what I did not understand. I began, however, to learn that

12\Breaking Through Barriers

the challenges that you face in life are not
always easy to explain or to understand.

Chapter 1
The Pain of Equal Rights

> "We hold these truths to be self-evident; that all men are created equal."
>
> Dr. Martin Luther King, Jr.

Chapter 1: The Pain of Equal Rights

I was just entering high school. It was the late 1960s, the time when schools across the country were slowly being desegregated. My parents had just received a notice in the mail that the children in our neighborhood were going to be bused next year to a nearby high school, which was historically White. To add to the news, it had been decided that the all-Black high school, where all of the neighborhood kids currently went, was going to be shut down the following year. The Black school had become overcrowded and too run down to keep open. Therefore, after this year, all of the high school students in our neighborhood would be bused to the fairly new White school.

A wave of fear and anger broke out in the neighborhood. People on both sides of the town were upset about the busing decision.

Although there were many mixed emotions about this issue, there was a common feeling throughout the town. Both Blacks and Whites feared that what was once a happy and complacent town would now break out into riots and endanger their lives. "If the White folks don't want us in their schools, then why should we force our way?" Blacks asked. "Besides, what gives them the right to close down *our* schools?" In the White neighborhood they asked, "Why do they want to change things? Aren't *they* happy where they are?"

As a child, this all seemed strange to me. The town was now in an uproar over something that many fought so hard to get. It was called "equal rights." It just did not add up at the time. I thought everyone would be excited about finally being treated fairly—about being treated equally. However, somewhere during all of the confusion, I began to understand what all of the fear and anxiety was about.

For the most part, my parents were pretty open-minded and believed that when doors are opened for you, you should take advantage of the opportunities that lie behind those doors. It sounded great until that day when I was faced with what I regarded as one of the toughest decisions of my life. My parents asked me if I wanted to attend the

White high school before the all-Black high school was shut down. Something hit the bottom of my stomach. I could not believe that they actually expected me to decide if I wanted to go to the White school during my first year of high school and leave my friends behind! "What a tough decision they've asked me, a child, to make!" I thought. "Did I really want to go to *their* school so soon or even at all? Why should I be the first to leave what I regarded as my family, *my roots* ?" I asked myself those questions over and over again. I now understood the fear and the anger that the town had voiced about the whole business of – *equal rights* !

Chapter 2

Can I Go On?

"Press forward. Do not stop, do not linger in your journey, but strive for the mark set before you."

George Whitefield

Chapter 2: Can I Go On?

IT is funny how the advice that your parents and loved ones give always seems to come back to haunt you. I often wondered if God planned it that way. It was almost time for the new school year to begin. I spent much of my summer worrying about which school I was going to attend and listening to lots of advice from my friends, relatives, and neighbors. It seemed as though everyone had something to say. Everyone had some advice to give, whether I asked for it or not.

Almost everyone felt that I should wait until the Black school closed. They were not concerned about me, but about their life. They said that if I went to the White school this year, it would only make the Whites angry. This could spark what they did not want to ever happen again in the neighborhood—more cross burnings! When I was about 9 years old, I remember seeing crosses that had been burned in one of our neighbor's yard. Fear ran rampart through the neighborhood. But, burning crosses was a thing of the past. Surely that would never happen again. Would it?

Listening to all of the advice only confused me. It finally came to a point that I knew what I had to do. I had to decide what would be best for me. My trying to make a decision was the hard part. How do you really know what is best for you? I was only a child! The words of my parents kept ringing in my ears—"whatever you do in life, keep it honest and always strive to do your best."

Although my parents were sure to let me know that they did not want me to feel pressured into going to the White school just to please them, I did feel somewhat pressured—pressured to do what I felt in my heart was right. I kept asking myself what was the real reason for not choosing to go to the White school a year ahead of everyone else. Was I going to let fear keep me from doing what I knew was right?

I was afraid, but I knew that I had to take a stand. I knew that my parents were counting on me to "try to strive to do my best." After many sleepless nights, I finally told them that I had decided to go to the White school this year. My parents were happy that I had made such a big decision and reminded me that I could change my mind at any time. My parents' support took some of the pressure off; but I knew deep down inside that they would have been disappointed if I had changed my mind.

Although my parents admired my courage, I also knew that they too were quite scared. Scared of what was going to happen to their child who had decided to pioneer into a clearly frightful world. Was this *really* the right decision for *their* child? Was it going to be worth the battle that they knew the family would soon go through?

News had quickly spread throughout the town that only two Black students had chosen to attend the White school during the first year that the schools were being desegregated—a boy from another part of town, whom I did not know, and little old me. I also learned that there were going to be about 800 White students attending school that year.

I remember praying hard the night before school started. My pillow, wet with tears, I asked God to watch over me and to protect me as I went onto my new journey in life. I often heard my grandmother and the people in church pray that prayer. I would always hear them say, "Dear Lord, please watch over us and keep us through life's journey." I really did not think much about what those words meant until now. Suddenly, those words had so much meaning. My grandmother said that God always answered her prayers. So, I thought I would give it a try. She also used to say, "Baby, just put your faith and trust in the Lord, and He will bring you through." Then, she would laugh and say, "Even a turtle has to stick his neck out to get somewhere."

"You're right grandma." I thought. "I *have* to go on!"

"The only impossible journey is the one you never begin."

Anthony Robbins

Chapter 3
You Don't Belong Here!

GO GO GO

"I am a person who believes in asking questions, in not conforming for the sake of conforming. I am deeply dissatisfied—about so many things, about injustice, about the way the world works - and in some ways, my dissatisfaction drives my storytelling."

Chimamanda Ngozi Adichie

Chapter 3: You Don't Belong Here!

IT seems like it was only yesterday. It was my first day of high school. My mother nervously peeked through the curtain as I waited for the school bus. She had offered to stand outside with me, but I told her "no." Besides, I was a teenager now and in high school. I did not want my mother or the kids in the neighborhood or those on the bus to think that I was *scared* ! No! I certainly could not project that image! Me scared? Only wimps did that! On the surface, I looked cool, but underneath I was *really* scared to death!

I was trembling from head to toe as I stepped onto the bus. I looked back at my house and wondered if I would ever see it again. I nervously said, "Good morning," to the bus driver. My parents always taught me to show good manners no matter what. They called it being respectful. The bus driver coldly nodded. I quickly found an empty seat near the front of the bus. It is where my mother told me to sit just in case I ran into any problems and had to exit quickly. Everything was going well apart from the stares and no one wanting to sit beside me. Then, it happened! One of the boys who just got on the bus hollered in a very Southern dialect from the back of the bus, "What's that n--ger doing here? Why don't you go back to where you belong!" Everyone laughed.

A cold chilling feeling came over me. I had heard that word used before, but no one had ever called me such a hurtful name. I just did not understand how anyone could be so cruel. I chose not to respond because I knew that was what they wanted me to do. So, I kept quiet and tried to ignore the ugly and hurtful words that they were all now chanting, "N--ger, go home. Go back to Africa." It was the longest bus ride that I ever had.

"It ain't what they call you, it's what you answer to."

W.C. Fields

Finally, I was at school! As I entered the school doors, I began to wonder if I had made a mistake. By now, I really *did* want to go back home! I wanted to go where I was welcomed—where I belonged. I began to understand what it felt like to not be accepted because I was different—not in the sense that I was strange or weird—but different in the sense that the color of my skin caused me to be an outcast. *Please note that you can substitute here anything that sets you apart from others—whether you are seen as being different because you are from another race or seen as being too short or too tall, too shy or too outgoing, too this or too that!*

As I found my way to my homeroom, no one bothered me. No one even talked to me. I was relieved. At least no one called me hurtful names. Everyone stared as I entered my homeroom—just like they were all deer looking into headlights. It became quite clear that I definitely *did not* belong.

There were times when I hated going to school. It was not because I did not like school, but because I always felt like I was a misfit. A typical day at school consisted of homeroom and eight classes. I would never talk to anyone, much less, make eye contact. I always had my homework, but never participated in the class discussions. My teachers appeared to be nice or maybe they just felt sorry for me. I only spoke when I was spoken to, which was hardly ever. I had become quite invisible. When it was time for lunch, I always had a table to myself. If I sat down at a table with other students (who were obviously White since there were only two Black students in the entire school), they would always get up and move to another table. Although this kind of treatment was horrible, I got used to it. Looking at the positive side of things—the isolation helped me to focus on my studies. I soon became a straight A student.

Chapter 4
Ding Dong, King Is Dead!

"Injustice anywhere is a threat to justice everywhere."

Dr. Martin Luther King, Jr.

Chapter 4: Ding Dong, King Is Dead!

As the school year went on, I learned to ignore the hurtful words that were spoken. I learned to tune them out since I practically heard them every day. Even the bus ride did not seem so horrible anymore. *Boy! An MP3 player or an Ipod would have come in handy back then. But remember, this was the 1960s. There were no cell phones, microwaves, or even school calculators!* At school, my teachers appeared to be nice. They always seemed to keep an eye on me. Of course, it was easy to do because I was the only Black child in my classes. Occasionally, I would see the other Black student in the hallways on the way to class. I did not even know his name. I later learned, however, that he was older and was in the tenth grade. We would sometimes make eye contact when we passed each other in the halls. At least there was the comfort of knowing that there was someone else like me in the school even though I did not ever get to talk to him.

Just when the school year seemed to be settling down, I received the most horrifying news ever! Dr. Martin Luther King, Jr. had been killed! What was I going to do! How would this affect me at a predominantly White school? Should I not go to school? Do I need an escort to protect me? Who would the escort be? My parents? They could not possibly go to school with me every day! Why did God let this happen? Now, I was really scared—scared for my life!

My parents decided to drive me to school for a few days. I knew that they could not take me to school the rest of the school year. At some point, I would have to get back on the bus. So, I asked my parents if I could resume riding the bus that week. They reluctantly agreed after talking to the principal to let him know their concerns for my safety. My parents were very vocal in the community about civil rights and were adamant about holding the principal and the school board accountable for any violent outbreaks towards me. I was still scared, but I felt better knowing that my parents were not afraid to stand up for what they believed. I suppose this sort of "no quit" attitude was instilled in me. Once again I was ready to face the unknown...but was I really?

Upon my return to riding the bus, all was well during the morning. There were no unusual outbreaks. "This is not so bad after all," I thought. The school day was even normal, relatively speaking of course. Well, it did not take me long to understand what my grandmother and the elders meant by the old adage "it's always quiet before the storm." As I got on the bus that afternoon, I noticed that the students were rowdier than usual. I took my seat and then it happened. They all began to chant to the tune of the *'Wicked Witch is Dead'* from *The Wizard of Oz* . They sang, "Ding, dong, King is dead. Clap your hands, King is dead. Ding, dong, n--ger King is dead." They were all celebrating the assassination of Dr. King. It was one of the saddest days of my life. I was sad not just because Dr. King had been killed, but because through ignorance and hatred people were cheering about the death of a man who stood up for the rights of all mankind—even for them, despite their stupidity. They continued to chant ugly words and began to throw paper and spitballs at me until I got off the bus. I was in tears—tears from anger and from sadness. How could they be so cruel!

My parents were both angry and upset about what happened. There was much discussion about what happened on the school bus. Their conversation continued into the night. They argued about whether they should take me out of the school for fear that my life would be threatened if they did not. My mother was angry because she was tired of seeing me come home crying and upset. My father believed in nonviolence, but my mother was tired of me getting beat up, both mentally and physically. In spite of their arguments and fears, I told them that I did not want to leave the school—that I *was not* going to let them make me quit! I now understood what Dr. King was trying to accomplish. I now clearly understood the importance of having civil rights. At that point, I knew why I could not give up. I could not give up the right to fight for what was mine all along—the opportunity to strive to do and be my best.

Chapter 5
The Fight is On!

> "Hate hurts the hater more than the hated, no matter how justified it may seem."
>
> *Randy Kilgore*

Chapter 5: The Fight is On!

THE next day my parents decided to take me to school and to talk to the principal about what had happened to me on the bus. My dad, who was a follower of Dr. King, was a very active civil rights leader in the community. The principal assured my father that I would be safe in his school and that he would not tolerate any more racial outbreaks. The principal called a school assembly to talk about what he expected from the students and what would happen if they did not behave. For the first time, I felt good about being in that school. Surprisingly, things settled down for quite some time after that. Even the kids on the bus seemed to behave—at least it seemed that way.

Almost two months had passed since Dr. King's death. They say time heals all wounds, I guess it does. I had begun to forget about how cruel the students acted when Dr. King was shot. The school year was almost over, and no one seemed to be bothering me. I wondered if they had gotten used to me.

In the mornings, I still managed to sit near the front of the bus. I would always have a seat to myself because no one wanted to sit beside me. I did not mind this—at least I had a seat. The afternoons were unpredictable, however. Sometimes all the seats would be occupied and I would either have to make someone let me sit beside them or stand up until an empty seat became available. One particular afternoon, the bus was crowded and I had to stand for a while. I could tell that the kids were up to something. They all began to snicker and whisper to a boy who stood up behind me before he got off the bus. I ignored them, as I always did. I ignored them until the boy decided to slap me on my butt as he passed by!

The boy touching me was the last straw! Immediately, I reacted! I slapped his face and began to choke him without thinking. I do not remember all of the details that took place afterwards, but the boy ran home crying with red marks around his throat. The other kids on the bus got quiet. They knew that I was mad and was ready to take them all on if I had to.

Although, I was afraid that my father would be upset, I told my parents what happened on the bus. My father did not believe in fighting. I knew that I could not take back what I had done and was willing to accept the consequences for my actions. Later that evening, the boy's father came to our house to discuss what I had done to *his poor* son. My father told him—in words that I never heard him use before— what he was going to do the next time his son decides to put his hands on me! Never before had I seen anyone turn so red and leave so angry! The man even threatened to sue us for hurting his son. To my knowledge, my parents never heard from him again, and I surely did not have any more trouble out of his son the rest of the year. I was very proud of my father that night. I later learned that he too was very proud of me. It was not because I chose to fight, but because I stood up for what was right.

Chapter 6

It's In My Blood?

(The Flashback)

"Stand up to your obstacles and do something about them. You will find that they haven't half the strength you think they have."

Norman Vincent Peale

Chapter 6: It's In My Blood?
(*The Flashback*)

MY father always believed in standing up for what he felt was right. Although my father was an advocate of nonviolence, he would go to great lengths to protect what belonged to him. It was a typical Saturday night during the summer. It was hot and humid. We used a window fan that continuously blew hot air to try to cool down the house. Of course, this was ineffective. So, we would go outside and sit on the porch to get relief from the heat.

As we sat on the porch that night, we watched the cars zoom back and forth. It was amazing how the drivers would toot their horns as they passed by—-this seemed to be part of that Southern hospitality wherein everyone takes the time to speak to each other whether or not they know each other. Being polite was just something that we did down

South, even when we drove pass people's houses.

Finally, it was cooling off. It was getting somewhat late in the night, about eleven o'clock. Fewer cars were passing by the house. The night had become very pleasant until my father saw a car coming down the road. The car slowed down at a neighbor's house a few yards away. He told us to quickly go into the house, turn off the lights, and stay away from the windows. My father got his shotgun and headed back on the porch. A carload of White boys were making their usual Saturday night drive-bys. The boys would throw firecrackers on the Blacks' porches or put them in their mailboxes. This prank was ritually done on Saturday nights to scare the Black folks. Remember, my father vowed to protect his family and property at all costs. As the car approached our house, my dad fired off the shotgun. The shots echoed like a cannon throughout the woods! All we could hear were tires peeling rubber as the car sped down the road.

To this day, I chuckle at what my dad did that night—how he stood up for what he believed was right. I now understand why I had to continue on my journey—-it was in my blood.

Chapter 7
Miracles Do Happen!

> "Impossible situations can become possible miracles."
>
> *Robert H. Schuller*

Chapter 7: Miracles Do Happen!

ANOTHER school year was about to start. The Black school was still open. I was still one of two Black students who decided to attend the White school. After having heard about the struggles that I faced during the school year, most of the Black parents were afraid to let their children go to the White school. They even wondered if I would be brave or *stupid* enough, as some boldly expressed, to go back.

After that first year, something was stirred up in me that would not let me quit. I *had* to go back. I now knew the meaning of the song that I often heard sung during the civil rights marches, *Ain't Gonna Let Nobody Turn Me Around*. I was determined that I was not going to let anyone keep me from going through the doors that had been opened for me.

So, I once again stood waiting for my school bus. I was not afraid this time. When my bus arrived, I proudly got on, greeted the bus driver, and took my usual seat. The bus driver had somewhat of a smile on his face. One that sort of said, "Welcome back." The bus began to fill up with new and familiar faces. I noticed that some of the troublemakers had graduated. The atmosphere seemed surprisingly peaceful. No one even seemed to stare at me like before, or maybe I just did not care to notice.

It was almost time for the meanest kid to get on the bus. This little girl always seemed to stir up the others. She was such a feisty little girl. As she got on the bus, she sat directly behind me. "Oh, great!" I thought. "She's really getting bold now. She's really asking for trouble." I braced myself and waited for her to start the taunting. My grandmother always told me that God answers prayers in his own time. Surely what happened next was a prayer answered. The little girl politely tapped me on the shoulder and said, "Good morning. I'm glad to see that you decided to come back. I'm sorry about the way I treated you last year. I was wrong. I spent the summer with my grandmother. She told me how wrong I had been and that God loves all of us, no matter what color we are. "

I could not believe my ears! The meanest kid was now being good? Miracles *do* happen! Hallelujah! The girl's actions were the turning point and the beginning of a new friendship. How could I be so forgiving after all I went through? Forgiving this little girl was a miracle within itself. It looked like this was going to be a good school year after all.

Chapter 8
Welcome Aboard?

"Out of difficulties grow miracles."

Jean de la Bruyere

Chapter 8: Welcome Aboard?

ANOTHER school year came and went. Surprisingly, there were no major upsets. As a matter of fact, although I still felt isolated, I learned that you cannot control other people's behavior. Now, it was time for another new school year to begin. I can truly say that for the first time, I was looking forward to going to school. The Black school had finally closed for good. Over 200 Black students were going to be bused to what I now claimed to be *my* school. I was so excited about this school year—excited because I would no longer be the only Black in my classes. I would no longer be the outcast. I would no longer be the only "X" among the "O's." At last, I would have someone in my school that was like me. Finally, I could fit into a society where I would be welcome. It was going to be the best school year ever, I thought.

I soon learned that there was another form of segregation. It was called "isolation." The Black students who had been *forced* to leave *their* schools to attend the *White* school did not take too kindly to me. I could not understand this. I could not understand why they did not like me when they did not even know me. Even my friends who grew up in my neighborhood started acting strange. I was upset about my friends' behavior. So, I shared how I felt with my parents. I'm so thankful that I could always talk to my parents about things that were bothering me. I told them that the Black students were treating me the same way that the White students did when I first went to high school. Can the Black students be prejudice too? Black students being prejudice was a concept that was too bizarre for me to understand. Black people couldn't possibly be prejudice against their own people, could they? Why and how could that happen?

After discussing this with my parents, I understood that the Black students were angry about being bused. Perhaps, they may have felt inferior and thought that I felt that I was *better* than they were. Perhaps, they even thought that I was no longer Black like they were—that I thought that I was *White* and that I had an advantage over them! Oh, how wrong they were in their thinking. If they could only count the tears that I cried or know about the many fears that I faced as I walked (as one of two Blacks in the entire school of about 800 Whites) down those very same halls that were now full of Black faces—smiling Black faces. It hurt me more to not be accepted by my own race than by being rejected by the Whites—at least I expected this kind of treatment from the Whites, but not from my own people. It was going to be another long, challenging school year.

Chapter 9
Time Heals All Wounds

"The difficulties of life are intended to make us better, not bitter."

Author Unknown

Chapter 9: Time Heals All Wounds

ALTHOUGH there were many challenges, the school year proved to be a year of growth. I learned what it meant to be part of the desegregation movement that changed the world. Gradually, the Black students started talking to me. They realized that they could learn from my experiences. They discovered that since I knew the teachers that were teaching their classes, it would be to their benefit to listen to what I had to say about them. I guess I became somewhat of a leader or an advocate for the Black students. Imagine that! At the beginning of the school year, they saw me as a threat, as someone who thought that I was "better than they were." As time progressed, they realized that this was the farthest thing from the truth. They discovered the benefits of having me as a friend. Yes, this whole concept sounds rather selfish, but let us face it...we *all* needed each other! I needed them to get rid of my feeling of isolation and they needed me to show them how to survive in a White world.

The school was still divided into Black and White. It was going to take a while for this feeling of division to diminish or to totally disappear. The Black students would see me in the cafeteria and share such concerns as them feeling mistreated or graded unfairly by the White teachers. I learned that sometimes these feelings were valid and sometimes they were not. Regardless, each person felt that his or her concerns were important enough to be heard. Often, I was just a sounding board. They would vent their frustrations, eat their lunches, and go back to their classes. I thought to myself, how I would have loved to have had someone to vent my frustrations to during that first year when there were no other Black students—except for that one Black boy whom I hardly ever saw.

I was so thankful that I no longer felt isolated or like an outcast by my own race. Time does indeed heal all wounds.

Chapter 10
The Homecoming Queen

"I learned that courage was not the absence of fear, but the triumph over it. The brave man is not he who does not feel afraid, but he who conquers that fear."
Nelson Mandela

Chapter 10: The Homecoming Queen

I was finally a junior! I was now *officially* an UPPER CLASSMAN! There were lots of activities to look forward to. Homecoming was coming up and the junior and senior prom would be in the spring. Homecoming meant that students would have to vote on a homecoming king and queen and their accompanying court. Well, this was going to be interesting since this would be the first time such an election would be held with both Black and White students voting. "Hmmm...now how is this going to work?" I thought.

The student council was very active that year and provided a way that students could submit their nominations for the homecoming election. The talk in the school that morning was that a Black girl had been nominated for homecoming queen along with a few other White nominees. I was shocked to hear this news, so I checked with my *reliable* sources to make sure that this was not just a rumor that someone was trying to start. I learned from past experiences how quickly people would try to pull the race card if given the opportunity. Also, I learned to not be so quick as to believe everything that I heard. After validating the information, I found out that it was true! A Black girl *had* been nominated! Wow! This was big! This was the first time the school would have an integrated homecoming ballot! What would this mean? The school year was going so well. I hoped that this would not cause a riot in the school. Students appeared to be getting along, but I could tell that it would not take a whole lot to bring back those memories of segregation, those memories of hatred.

The principal was going to make the announcement about the homecoming ballot during homeroom period before we went to our classes. I actually thought that it would be better to make that announcement at the end of the day—right before the students go home. Oh well, it was too late. The principal came on the intercom and first started congratulating the nominees. As he called out the names, I thought that I was in a dream or *nightmare* when I heard my name. I could not believe it! I did not know whether to cry, scream, or just run out of the classroom! I had no idea that I was being nominated. No one ever asked me if I wanted to be nominated. I guess they knew that my answer was going to be "No!" So, what should I do? Apparently, someone thought enough of me to nominate me. I did not want to disappoint them. But, I certainly didn't want to go through this whole election thing either. Being involved with the election just was not my cup of tea!

The students (both Black and White) congratulated me that day. Politely, I thanked them—but if they only knew how scared and upset I was about the whole homecoming election. What if I do not win? Or worse yet, what if I win? Either way, the mere thought of my name being on that ballot caused me much angst.

I went home quite upset that day. As my parents calmed me down, they said something to me that would stick with me the rest of my life. They told me that whether I win or lose, the fact that I tried is what matters and that they were proud of me regardless. The next day, I went to school with a different attitude—a better attitude about myself and about my purpose in life.

The election was held. The votes were in and counted. No, I did not become the first Black homecoming queen. But, I was runner-up! I was the first Black student to be a part of the school's homecoming court. I will forever remember that homecoming night! My mother, who is a seamstress, made my homecoming outfit. It was beautiful. I wore a yellow, laced gown with chiffon sleeves and a matching formal coat. My parents were so proud when I stepped onto that football field in front of all of those people. When I saw the looks on my parents' faces, I knew that my struggles were not in vain. I am forever grateful for the time that they invested in me. They gave me a foundation that is priceless— a lifetime of core values that I will forever cherish.

Well, my participation in homecoming seemed to help tear down some lingering racial barriers. The students were friendlier toward each other. The racial divide in the school was beginning to become less prominent. We began sitting at lunch tables and participating in after-school activities together. We really came a long way that year.

Homecoming came and went. It was now spring. It was prom time! For most of the students, the prom brought the excitement of finding a date, putting together the outfit that makes a statement when you walk into the room, decorating the gym, and just feeling all grown up! There was something about a prom event that brought even the most dysfunctional group of people together.

As the prom committees were formed, the Black and White barriers seemed to diminish. These barriers did not totally disappear, mind you. However, the students worked together for the event without any obvious issues. It was great! There was a lot of discussion about the theme of the prom, the colors, the food, the music, and all other prom matters that arose. Amazingly, things went smoothly. No, seriously they did. The students respectfully expressed their ideas and got the job done. We had a great prom!

Chapter 11
But I'm Number One!

"We may encounter many defeats, but we must not be defeated."

Dr. Maya Angelou

Chapter 11: But I'm Number One!

IT is my Senior year! I finally like school, the students, the teachers, the whole package. I now have friends with whom I have bonded. I was finally feeling on top of the world. I no longer rode the bus because I was now driving my own car to school! No, it was not a brand new car. It was a used Rambler that I nicknamed "Biscuit." My uncle had an auto shop and overhauled the car so that I could use it to go to and from school. It was really nice of him. My family was and still is supportive of one another. I am so grateful that I have that kind of support.

As a Senior, I now had more flexibility. I had taken most of my core courses and was waiting to hear from the colleges to which I had applied. My guidance counselor insisted that I apply to the College of William and Mary since that was her alma mater. But, the thought of me starting all over again in a predominantly White school was frightening. After much discussion with my parents, I decided to apply to William and Mary and to Hampton Institute (now Hampton University). What a contrast—a prestigious historically White Ivy league school versus a prestigious historically Black college! My guidance counselor (who was White) could not understand why I wanted to apply to Hampton Institute. After all, she felt that "they" had "groomed" me to become the student who could probably get accepted into the top colleges—so why waste my potential by applying elsewhere? No, she did not come right out and say this to my face, but I could tell that this was what she was thinking based on her body language and facial expressions as we talked. So to satisfy my counselor, I applied to her alma mater as well. From my discussions with my parents about this, I knew that the final decision would be mine anyway. So, it would not hurt to apply to William and Mary.

My Senior year ended up becoming another year of growth. In addition to waiting for college decisions, there were the student rankings. Who would be the top two students for my graduating class? Who would be "Valedictorian" and "Salutatorian" for the class of 1972?

The talk in the school was that I had the highest overall grade-point average in my class. However, there was another student (a White girl who actually became a close friend over the years) who was also an "A" student. So how was this going to work? Would there be two Valedictorians?

Although the racial divide in the school had seemingly died down over the past couple of years, it did not take much to re-kindle the fire. Quite a stir had developed over who was going to be ranked number one!

After a few weeks of hype, the rankings were finally announced. My friend and I had the same GPAs! We were both individually called into the guidance counselor's office where we received the news. The counselor and the school principal had decided to make my friend the class Valedictorian! I was shocked! So, I asked why. They explained that it was a hard decision. However, because my friend had taken Latin and I had taken French, they felt that Latin was a more viable language and carried more weight. Yes, they changed the rules to fit their desired outcome!

I left the counselor's office very upset! My friend saw me later that day and told me that she disagreed with the decision and apologized. It was a very civil act of kindness on her part. However, it did not remove the hurt that I felt. All the years of supposedly gaining *equal rights* and *fairness* just died! The news about what had happened regarding the class rankings spread through the school like a wildfire.

The school was in a racial uproar once again! One thing that I have learned through my journey is that racial injustices impact everyone. Over the years, the Blacks and Whites had developed great friendships at school. Regardless of skin color, an injustice was an injustice. There were just as many White students as Black students who were protesting the ranking decision. This was indeed an eye opener for me.

Students were no longer passive. They were no longer afraid to speak out about injustices. I heard many of the White students openly speak to the principal and counselors in student government meetings about the (unjust) decision that they made.

So, what was the result of this uproar? My parents decided to meet with the Board of Education about this issue. No, my parents did not mess around! They were serious about standing up for what they believed. I suppose that is where I get my drive for justice and fairness.

After they met with the Board, the decision was to no longer have titles for student rankings. There would be no more "Valedictorian" or "Salutatorian" labels.

Instead, since my friend and I had the same GPAs, the top three students of the class of 1972 would be recognized and allowed to speak at the commencement ceremony. Was this a fair decision or a cop-out? Was this a "win-win" solution? Well, although I did not like the *unjust* reasoning that led up to the school board's final decision, the fact that I actually got to see how the support from both sides (Black and White students) evolved was a victory.

Chapter 12
The Great News!

"You can't make decisions based on fear and the possibility of what might happen."

Michelle Obama

Chapter 12: The Great News!

MY college decision letters arrived! I met with my guidance counselor to inform her of my decision. She was elated that I had been accepted by both Hampton Institute/University and the College of William and Mary. Apparently, she was sure that I was going to attend her alma mater. However, I selected Hampton Institute. My counselor questioned why I selected Hampton. I could see the disappointment on her face as she tried to convince me of the pros and cons about my decision. The more she talked, the more convinced I became that I had made the right choice.

As she talked, I began to reflect on the struggles and the pain from all of the injustices that I had faced throughout high school. I reflected on how I had endured such a difficult journey. She made me realize that I had enough and that it was time for a new beginning—a new journey. I knew that I needed time to heal—that I needed time to overcome all of the hurt and pain that had built up over the years. I had to learn to love and to forgive those who had tried to crush my very being.

"Turn your wounds into wisdom."

Oprah Winfrey

Chapter 1
The Beginning of a New Journey

I look to the hills from whence cometh my help. Where does my help come from? My help comes from the Lord, the maker of heaven and earth ...Psalm 121

"The most important lesson that I have learned is to trust God in every circumstance. Lots of times we go through different trials and following God's plan seems like it doesn't make any sense at all. God is always in control and He will never leave us."

Allyson Felix

Chapter 1: The Beginning of a New Journey

AFTER I graduated from high school, I started to reflect on the lessons that I learned from my past. I no longer questioned God about why as a child He allowed me to go through so much turmoil. Over time, I realized that God had a clear purpose for my life. All I needed to do was to agree to have enough faith in Him to walk in that purpose. Did I understand what was happening at that time? Of course not! Did I like the challenges, the struggles? Absolutely not! I hated my life during that period of time. But, I learned that in order to move forward, I had to learn to bury the past and glean from it the blessings. The blessings? How could I see the blessings from being hated and mistreated because I looked different from the majority? How could I overcome the inequities and the barriers that I continued to face? I learned that only God could help me get through such times. I had to make sure that as I moved on to the next phase of my life, I did not harbor bitterness and anger. I had to make sure that I did not become like the individuals that I had struggled so hard to rise above. A writer once said that *"Hate hurts the hater more than the hated, no matter how justified it may seem."*[1]

So I decided to release my past, to forgive, and begin a new journey.

---

[1] Randy Kilgore,. Our Daily Bread, "Outlasting Bitterness," November 23, 2014.

"Your journey has molded you for the greater good. It was exactly what it needed to be. Don't think you've lost time. It took each and every situation you have encountered to bring you to the now, and now is right on time."

Asha Tyson

About the Author

The author is a scientist at the National Institute of Standards and Technology where she has worked for over 30 years. Her college education began at Hampton Institute (now Hampton University) located in Hampton, Virginia where she majored in Chemistry. She received a Master of Business Administration from Frostburg State University in Frostburg, Maryland. She humbly credits all that she has accomplished to Jesus Christ, her parents, her grandmothers Mrs. Clara Mitchell Beamon and Mrs. Alberta Reid Brown. Two years after starting her career in Maryland, she met her husband who she thought was a Marylander. However, she later discovered that he was actually from Virginia and had lived only 45 minutes from her hometown. She and her husband now have four beautiful children, three wonderful grandsons, and one very talented Goddaughter. As strange as it may seem, the author is forever grateful for the struggles that God allowed her to endure. It is because of these childhood challenges, she can share her story with others.